What makes Cornwall different?

Paul White

Bossiney Books · Exeter

Calstock on the Tamar, with a railway viaduct dating from 1908, carrying Tamar Valley Line from Plymouth to Gunnislake

First published 2023 by
Bossiney Books Ltd, 68 Thorndale Courts, Whitycombe Way,
Exeter, EX4 2NY

www.bossineybooks.com

© 2023 PaulWhite All rights reserved
ISBN 978-1-915664-27-3

The photographs are by Robert Hesketh (roberthesketh.co.uk) or by the author.

Printed in Great Britain by Deltor, Saltash, Cornwall

Introduction

Anyone planning a first visit to Cornwall, and looking at a map, cannot help but think that there must be something special about this peninsula, some 80 miles (130 km) long, separated from Devon by the Tamar and getting steadily narrower towards Land's End. And when actually entering Conwall from the East, that impression is immediately confirmed by place names in the Cornish language – Tregadillet, Polyphant, Langore and Egloskerry if you arrive by the A30, Trematon, Botusfleming, Landrake and Polbathic if you arrive by the A38. But if you enter from the North, for the first few miles the place names remain mostly 'English' – Kilkhampton, Marhamchurch, Stratton.

What makes Cornwall different? The answer lies in its geography and geology. These in combination influenced its history, including the story of the Cornish language, once dominant but now spoken only by a few proud preservers. Until Tudor times Cornwall was in effect a separate country west of the Tamar, called Kernow, but as the place names demonstrate, the northern border, for the language at least, was the River Ottery.

Differences by geography

Being surrounded by sea now makes Cornwall seem isolated. But this apparent isolation is due to our modern assumption that access is by land. Before 1800 there were no good roads: access by sea meant that Cornwall was one of the *least* isolated parts of Britain. Phoenicians, Greeks and Romans had visited and traded; there was much contact with Brittany, and the port of Fowey had traded farther afield. From Tudor times, Falmouth became the key port for contact with the Mediterranean, with Royal Mail packet ships based there.

That same easy access was also a vulnerabilty. South Cornwall in particular suffered raids during England's wars with France and Spain, and during the seventeenth and early eighteenth centuries North African pirates captured thousands of Cornish people and made them slaves.

Fishing

Agricultural land in Cornwall is relatively poor, with little arable and large areas of rough moorland. With sea all around them, it is unsurprising that from earliest times the population turned to fishing, and to collecting shellfish from the shore. The result today is numerous coastal communities which have, or used to have, fishing as their main activity, ranging from coves with just a landing ramp to Newlyn, which over the centuries has grown into one of the most productive fishing ports in England. This contrasts with John Leland's account in 1542 (spelling modernised):

> Newlyn is a hamlet belonging to Mousehole which is a pretty fisher town in the West part of Mount's Bay, lying hard by the shore, and has no safeguard for ships but a forced [artificial] pier. Penzance, about a mile [actually 3 miles] from Mousehole, on the shore of Mount's Bay, is the westernmost market town of all Cornwall, and has no succour for boats or ships but a forced pier or quay.

Newlyn harbour

Cadgwith on the Lizard, one of many small but active fishing harbours

The ancient fishing harbours of Cornwall are one of its chief attractions, with towns such as St Ives, Padstow and Looe, and smaller harbours such as Port Isaac, Boscastle, Polperro, Mevagissey, Cadgwith and Mousehole. The fish caught have varied over the years: these days crabs and lobsters are important, but from 1700 to about 1880 the most important catch was pilchards (recently re-branded as 'Cornish sardines'). There were two competing methods of catching them, by seine nets or drifters.

Drifters were owned by individual fishermen; they went further out to sea, but they took a small proportion of the total catch. Seine nets were huge, at least 300 metres in length, and consequently very expensive. They were usually the property of a local landowner or wealthy merchant so, unlike drifting, seining was a capitalist enterprise.

A 'huer' was employed to watch the sea, sometimes from a watch tower such as survives at Newquay. When a shoal of pilchards was spotted, the huer shouted 'Hevva!' and people dropped what they were doing; the men rushed to the shore, and the women to the cellars where the catch would be processed. The huer directed activities by a kind of semaphore. Boats took the net out and attempted to surround the shoal: then the net was pulled towards the beach and smaller boats went within the net to bring the fish ashore.

Catches were intermittent – a seine might take just one catch in a season – but they could be enormous. The largest day's catch at St Ives was in 1847, when over 57 million pilchards were taken, which rather exceeded the local demand! The fish were taken to specialist buildings where they were gutted and, over a five week period, salted. The bulk of it was then exported, particularly to Italy, and it was such a huge trade that there were more than 40 vessels, sailing mostly from Falmouth.

Before the construction of decent roads, Boscastle was a port for Launceston and much of North Cornwall

Access by land

Until the early 19th century, there was a complete lack of anything we would describe as a road. Wheeled vehicles were almost unknown, except for a few pretentious gentry carriages. Goods were transported by packhorses. Whilst road transport improved to some extent from the early 1800s, it was still inefficient.

It was the arrival of a railway connection which made a huge difference. There had been very early industrial railways within Cornwall, but the connection with the rest of the country only happened with the opening of Brunel's Royal Albert Bridge in 1859.

Suddenly fresh Cornish products could be transported to London overnight. This made a huge difference to the Newlyn fish market, and also to market gardeners. Cornish new potatoes and Cornish daffodils were soon on sale across the country. And of course the arrival of the railway also started the tourist industry.

Differences by geology

A great chain of granite outcrops runs from Scilly to Dartmoor, and has had a profound effect on Cornwall's history. On the edges of the granite, numerous valuable minerals are found – not just the tin and copper for which Cornwall is famous, but many other minerals which have had different values through the ages, including uranium, zinc, manganese, arsenic and china clay (kaolin). In North Cornwall slate is found. All these minerals have been subject to mining or quarrying, and these were for centuries Cornwall's source of wealth, though there is no mining now. The latest prize is lithium, an element much in demand for the batteries required for electric cars, etc, and preparations are in hand for extracting it in liquid form.

The Lizard peninsula, strangely sticking out from the main Cornish peninsula, is geologically different from anywhere else in Britain, and includes areas of serpentine rock. Apparently the Lizard was once quite separate from the rest of Britain but in Continental drift about 300 million years ago it was knocked off one of the super-continents then breezing around, and it got stuck on Cornwall. The serpentine soil of the Lizard is home to many unusual plants. It is a fantastic area to explore.

Mining

Mineral extraction was a crucial part of the Cornish economy from ancient times, first in the form of 'streaming' where small pieces of tin ore which had been swept down into valleys were separated out and washed before being smelted. This process left little impression on the landscape. Underground mining started in the late Middle Ages, and had a more serious impact.

There are many old mining areas in Britain, and most of them still show signs of the detrimental impact the industry had, with slag heaps as well as bland areas where slag heaps have been bulldozed away. Are there any areas of Britain other than Cornwall where the mining landscape is now a source of tourist interest?

Two factors make Cornwall different in this way: the characteristic Cornish engine house, used for pumping water from the mines and

An engine house at Botallack, with others in the distance

raising the ore, and the fact that a number of mines were situated along the coast, so that engine houses and cliffs in combination create a dramatic picture.

The engine houses were first designed for the earliest kind of steam engine, around 1710: the engines underwent improvements (by James Watt and a number of rivals) but the engine house remained much the same until the near collapse of tin and copper mining in the 1870s caused most Cornish mines to close. Mines that survived into the 20th century adopted different kinds of power, which is why, in British coal-mining areas, their early engine houses were replaced by later buildings.

In some areas, for example Dartmoor, which is geologically similar to Cornwall, abundant water power made steam pumping engines unnecessary: Dartmoor has just one Cornish engine house, though a very fine example, Wheal Betsy. The Bossiney title *Cornish Engine*

Houses explains their history in more detail and gives suggestions for visits to mining sites and scenic walks.

Just how ancient is Cornish mineral extraction? A relatively recent clue came in 2010, when the Nebra Sky Disk, found in Germany, was analysed. The disk itself is irrelevant to this book (though its Wikipedia article is fascinating): its significance is that the gold in the disk came from the River Carnon, and the tin in its bronze was also Cornish. The disk is dated to between 1800 and 1600 BC. So extraction is at least that old, and probably even older.

Quarrying and open-cast mining

There have been many materials quarried in Cornwall, but four stand out: granite, china clay, serpentine and slate.

The largest working granite quarry is the De Lank quarry at Hantergantick near St Breward, which produces a particularly fine quality – the Royal Opera House, Covent Garden, was built from De Lank stone.

China clay (kaolin) was discovered in Cornwall in 1746 by a Devonshire chemist, William Cookworthy. Kaolin was used in China to make porcelain, which was fetching huge prices in the British market: Cookworthy promptly set up the Plymouth China Factory. The deposits near St Austell turned out to be the largest so far discovered in the world, and Cornish china clay became a global industry. Uses for china clay also expanded. It is used in pills, toothpaste, rubber, lightbulbs and the paper which forms the book you are reading. Over a period of 250 years, this district produced 170 million tonnes of china clay. While Cornwall still produces some china clay, world production has moved to Brazil, where an even larger deposit was found – and where wages are cheaper.

The huge slag heaps used to be bright white, so much so that they became known as the Cornish Alps. Today vegetation is beginning to recover in an area which was a classic case of human devastation. For the visitor today, there are the Wheal Martyn museum, the port of Charlestown, which was built for the export of china clay and remains relatively unspoilt, and the Eden Project which flourishes on the site of former china clay pits.

Remains of a slate quarry between Tintagel and Trebarwith Strand

Serpentine became very popular in the Victorian period for making vases, largely because of the encouragement of Prince Albert, who came ashore during a cruise round the Cornish coast and was impressed. A few craftsmen on the Lizard continue to work it.

Slate is found in North Cornwall, where the huge Delabole slate quarry has a history going back to the 15th century, if not earlier. It is still working, but on a very small scale compared to the past, because Welsh slate is cheaper. There were many other quarries in the area, which used the miniature 'ports' of Tintagel and Port Gaverne. For the visitor today, the most attractive feature is probably the coastpath walk south from Tintagel to Trebarwith Strand: slate used to be quarried from the cliffs, and some strange rock shapes remain, presumably because they were of a inferior quality.

Other strange rock formations

If some strange rock formations are the work of man, many others in Cornwall are totally natural. There are some fine examples along the coast, and others on Bodmin Moor. One curious feature is the 'logan stones', of which there are several examples and there used to be more. A large rock is balanced above a supporting rock, but so loosely that it can be rocked ('logan' being dialect for 'to rock').

As with many other formations, 18th century antiquarians thought it likely that logan stones were not natural, but that 'the Druids' had constructed them. William Borlase in his *Antiquities, Historical and Monumental, of the County of Cornwall*, published in 1769, says that these structures

> may with great probability, I think, though of such stupendous weight, be asserted to be the works of Art, the under-stones in some instances appearing to have been fitted to receive and support the upper one. It is also plain, from their works at Stonehenge and other monuments, that the Druids had skill enough in mechanical powers to lift vast weights; and the Ancients, we know, in these rude works, spared no labour to accomplish their design.

Opposite: the Tolmen at Constantine, as illustrated in Borlase's book
Above: the Cheesewring on Bodmin Moor

Borlase was referring to the Tolmen at Constantine, West of Falmouth, which he measured as 33 ft long and 14 ft 6 in deep, which no longer exists. It was knocked off its support by a deliberate explosion in 1869, then fell 40 ft into the quarry. A miner named Thomas Dunstan was responsible: the owner of the quarry denied all responsibility....

'The Irish Lady'. Legend says that an Irish ship was wrecked and all on board drowned, except one woman who was seen on this rock. But she could not be rescued, and died some days later. Her ghost was occasionally seen, sitting on the rock

Borlase also considered the Cheesewring on Bodmin Moor, but decided that unlike the Tolmen it was probably natural.

A fuller account of such antiquarian speculations can be found in *Druids in the South-West?* The most famous logan stone today is at Treryn Dinas in West Penwith, photo opposite.

St Michael's Mount is perhaps less strange than it might at first appear. It is a hill turned into an island by rising sea levels, and its Cornish name translates as 'hoar rock in woodland'; at very low tides signs of ancient woodland have been seen in the bay.

Above: One of nature's sculptures, at Trewavas east of Mount's Bay

Below: Treryn Dinas headland, above Pedn Vounder beach

A different history

Prehistory

The antiquarians were understandably fascinated by the large number of prehistoric ('Druidic' as they imagined) structures found in Cornwall – stone circles, 'quoits', standing stones, etc – in far greater numbers than in most other areas of Britain. (This is another feature in which Cornwall's moors and Dartmoor share a 'difference'.) Speculation suggests two reasons: firstly, that on the high and treeless ground they were built of stone, whereas perhaps on lower ground comparable structures were of wood and have rotted away; and secondly, that they have survived on high ground little favoured for habitation, whereas lower down stone has been in greater demand, and prehistoric sites have been cannibalised for farm buildings or gate posts. In Cornwall, the greatest numbers are found on high moorland in West Penwith and on Bodmin Moor.

Among the earliest structures are the 'quoits', elsewhere called chamber tombs, which date from 3500 to 2500 BC. Most are in Penwith but one of the finest is Trethevy Quoit, on the southern edge of Bodmin Moor (SX 259688).

Trethevy Quoit

Stannon stone circle on Bodmin Moor

Of the stone circles, which are thought to date between 2500 and 1600 BC, I would particularly recommend Boscawen-ûn (SW 410277) in West Penwith; the Hurlers (a set of three circles) in the south of Bodmin Moor at Minions (SX 258714); and Fernacre (SX 145799) and Stannon (SX 125800) both in the north of Bodmin Moor. Several walks in *Shortish Walks on Bodmin Moor* visit these circles and other nearby antiquities including Bronze Age villages.

From the Romans to the Stuarts

When the Romans invaded in AD 43, most of Britain shared a common 'Brythonic' language, doubtless with local dialects, but there were numerous separate statelets. Some of these opposed the Romans, others accepted or even welcomed them. Cornwall seems to have made no resistance, and the Romans were probably happy to establish good relations with an area of such considerable mineral wealth.

A fort large enough for a whole legion has recently been found at Roche, but seems to have been occupied for weeks at most. There is also a Roman fort at Nanstallon, but it does not suggest an occupation force. In fact there is little evidence of Romanisation at all in Cornwall.

Much more significant is what happened more than a century after the Romans left, with the old statelets reappearing and England becoming 'Saxon'.

Launceston Castle, a Norman stronghold

There is much academic argument about how many actual Saxon immigrants there were, and there certainly wasn't a genocide. It seems likely that, whereas in the Roman period many of the wealthier inhabitants of England, especially urban merchants, would have spoken Latin, by the sixth century the dominant economic language was Anglo-Saxon. It was a language change rather than a genetic one.

But Cornwall and Wales continued speaking their Brythonic languages, and as Wessex enlarged in area and confronted Cornwall, there were local wars. A border formed along the length of the Tamar. In the north of Cornwall, the linguistic boundary can be seen from the place names. To the south of the River Ottery the names are largely Cornish, with Tre- a common element. To its north there are more places ending in -ton or -worthy, both of which meant much the same as Tre-.

Strong connections developed between Cornwall and both Brittany and Ireland, and many people from Cornwall and parts of Devon seem to have emigrated to Brittany, which ceased to be called Armorica and became *Bretagne* or 'Little Britain'. The Breton and Cornish languages are closely related.

Cornwall was not subdued by its eastern neighbours until AD 838, but even then it remained 'a land apart'. Kernow was regarded as a separate country from England, just as Wales was, until at least the Tudor period, and it is no coincidence that eldest son of the British monarch becomes both Prince of Wales and Duke of Cornwall. It was an acknowledgement by the Crown of its separate sovereignty over these countries. The Duchy of Cornwall was established by Edward III in 1337 to provide a separate income for his son and heir.

In 1500 then, the Cornish people knew they were different, and felt secure. Whilst officially part of England, they were under a different constitution and Kernow was widely recognised as a separate country. With their separate language, the Cornish were, in the idiom of that time, seen as a separate race. What changed this?

Use of the language had already declined, and would decline further. As so often happens, an economically dominant language has the advantage. Initially in the east of the county, especially in border areas near Saltash or Launceston, bilingualism probably became common, and mono-lingualism soon followed. And across a much wider area, the gentry in particular would have spoken English in 'polite' society.

A catastrophic event occurred in 1549. It was a tenet of Protestantism that people should hear the word of God in their own tongue. Edward VI's new government decreed that the Latin prayerbook should be replaced by an English one. A huge West Country rebellion broke out, partly in support of Catholicism but, in western Cornwall, because English was *not* their own tongue.

The rebellion was suppressed and thousands died. Governments would remain suspicious of Cornwall for some time thereafter.

The language retreated still further west. But despite that, Cornish 'difference' held firm across the county. In the English Civil War, the Cornish supported the King. The King lost, and both Cornwall's identity and its language were further weakened as a result; by the late 18th century the language appeared to be dead.

But it would be revived in the 20th century: Cornwall has a small but strong national movement, and language and identity remain closely allied.

Some 'differences' in early modern Cornish history

The consequences of an exposed coast

In peacetime a lengthy coast was an advantage for fishing, for trade and for 'free trade' (smuggling) but, in times of war or piracy, living near the coast was a hazard. Towards the end of the Hundred Years War, in 1457, there was a French attack on Fowey. This was an understandable military target, because Fowey had become a centre for pirates, sometimes licensed as 'privateers', who raided the French coast. During a six week siege, Lady Elizabeth Treffry, in the absence of her husband, defended Place House, allegedly by pouring down boiling lead stripped from the roof.

Doubtless there were lesser events, but the next serious attack was the Spanish raid on Mount's Bay in 1597, when they destroyed Mousehole, Paul (including its church), Newlyn and Penzance, looting and burning. There was no obvious military objective for this except revenge for the Armada disaster. Mount's Bay was just the easiest target: the Fal estuary was by then much more important, but Henry VIII had defended it with impressive forts (still there) at St Mawes and Pendennis.

Mousehole harbour

St Mawes Castle

In the 17th and 18th centuries another enemy was regularly present – the 'barbary pirates' who were based in North Africa, but whom the Government called 'Turks'. In 1625 a Government minute notes 'The Turks are upon our coasts. They take ships only to take the men to make slaves of them.' As many as 60 pirate ships were around the coasts of Cornwall and Devon at any one time. In addition to taking English ships, they raided coastal settlements such as St Keverne and Mousehole, and took women and children as well as sailors. The captives were either ransomed (for about £30 per head, a huge amount then) or sold into slavery in the Ottoman empire, where the men would become galley-slaves. In 1640 there were 3–5000 English captives in Algiers alone, hoping, mostly in vain, to be ransomed.

After the French Revolution, Cornwall was again under threat. A French invasion of Britain was planned, but where would they land? One option was to start from a vulnerable outpost such as Cornwall, and use it as a base for a wider attack.

In 1797 a French attack on Cornwall actually was planned, though intended as a diversion from the main attack, which was to be in Ireland. Two more diversionary attacks were planned at the same time. In the event, the Cornish invasion was cancelled, stormy weather prevented the landings in Ireland and near Newcastle, and the only invasion, at Fishguard in Pembrokeshire, was soon defeated.

Smuggling

Many coastal areas of Britain have been involved in smuggling, but none more famously than Cornwall. The peak of the smuggling industry was from 1700 to 1850, due to taxation of imports, but in the Middle Ages taxation of exports was in force. Wool was smuggled from Devon, and tin from Cornwall. Miners were required to take their tin to a 'stannary town' and sell it to the Duchy of Cornwall – at a price set by the Duchy. Unsurprisingly, much tin, probably more than half, was quietly taken to the coast and disappeared.

A revenue cutter, with a fishing/smuggling lugger behind it

The surge in smuggling began with the imposition in the 1690s of increased duties on imported goods, to pay for numerous wars, mostly with France. The upper classes were strongly against income tax, because they would have had to pay most of it, so taxes ('duties') on imported goods were the norm. As well as spirits, there were taxes on tea, silks, tobacco, and in the end no fewer than 1400 other items.

People of all classes strongly resented the price rises which resulted, and had no moral quibbles about buying cheaper smuggled goods. In coastal areas they were also delighted by the opportunity to make money out of the trade.

Gentry and clergy funded the industry: fishermen were already equipped for it on a small scale, and if somebody would only provide larger boats they could expand the industry. Badly paid agricultural workers and, in Cornwall, miners, were more than happy to spend a night landing a cargo and hiding it. A wide network watched out for activity by the preventive services. Members of those services were themselves often happy to turn a blind eye in return for a share of the profits.

Smugglers were an integral part of the community, as much in Devon and Dorset coastal areas as in Cornwall. What made Cornwall different was that nowhere is far from the coast, even central places such as Jamaica Inn. Rudyard Kipling summed it up:

> Them that asks no questions isn't told a lie,
> Watch the wall my darling, while the Gentlemen go by!
> Five and twenty ponies
> Trotting through the dark –
> Brandy for the Parson,
> 'Baccy for the Clerk

Not to mention profits for the squire.

Each smuggling area had its own specialities, especially in spirits. Kent and East Sussex, so near the Continent and London, specialised in cheap gin, Morecambe Bay in Irish whiskey. Both Devon and Cornwall traded extensively with the Channel Islands for French brandy (*cognac*, anglicised as 'Cousin Jack') and when the English government tried to stop this, the French followed up by making what

Mevagissey was heavily involved in smuggling

was then the village of Roscoff a 'free port'. Cornish merchants (along with Scots and Irish) settled in Roscoff, which grew rapidly into a substantial town dedicated to supplying the smuggling industry.

As the south-westernmost point of Britain, Cornwall had a particular advantage. East Indiamen, both British and Dutch, were returning from the east and heading up the Channel carrying highly taxed goods, such as tea and silks. Their captains were all too happy to stop on their way and sell much of their cargo to Cornish smugglers. And ships from the Caribbean and America heading up the north coast towards the Bristol Channel were equally happy to take a pause: their goods included sugar, tobacco and rum.

'Legitimate' merchants in Falmouth were happy to purchase smuggled goods and then ship them onward to London or other markets.

Cornwall was also fortunate to have an off-shore smuggling warehouse, called the Isles of Scilly. (Devon's equivalent was Lundy.) There was a large market for rum for the Navy's ships in Plymouth, serviced by smuggling in small boats from Scilly to Cawsand/Kingsand.

Two things brought this period of the smuggling industry to a close (though of course smuggling has never been entirely suppressed). In the 18th century the preventive services had been out-sourced, which was inefficient: the government finally took control and, after a period of bad management, in 1822 the Coastguard became highly efficient.

But the real break-through was in the 1840s, when import duties were reduced to a point where smuggling ceased to be profitable.

Mining and the industrial revolution

The arrival of the first Boulton & Watt steam engines in Cornwall, around 1780, had an enormous effect. The old Newcomen engines had required far too much coal, which had to be transported expensively from South Wales. But the atmosphere in mining also changed: Cornwall was suddenly full of people with new ideas (see *Cornwall's*

Dolcoath mine

Engineers and Inventors). Watt's 1769 patent was frustrating to many of them, as they came up with potential improvements which they were not allowed to make.

Once the patent expired in 1800, they could enact their dreams – in Trevithick's case producing the world's first working steam locomotive in 1804. At one time there were more than 600 steam engines working Corwall's mines – mainly for tin, since Parys Mountain in Anglesey dominated copper at that time.

Miners were paid by the 'tribute system', which meant receiving a proportion of the value of what they extracted. Every ninth Saturday there was a kind of auction, in which groups of miners (between two and eight, called a 'pare') would bid for the right to work specific areas. Success depended not just on hard work for nine weeks, but on having made the right bet in the first place. Each pare was in effect a small business, and Cornish miners are said to have been particularly independent and resourceful as a consequence.

They needed to be, because the industry was periodically struck by falls in the price fetched by the ore, and in the 1870s the Cornish industry almost failed totally as cheaper tin from Malaysia and Australia took over the market. Huge numbers emigrated from Cornwall, a quarter of a million between 1861 and 1901, disproportionately male, disproportionately skilled miners moving to the new mining areas. The 'Cornish diapora' can be found living in many countries across the world.

While mining itself was challenged, the local engineering firms which had developed specialised mining equipment would thrive on exports for many decades more – but poverty was widespread in late Victorian Cornwall.

Tourism

The answer – or is it? – was tourism.

Mass tourism began with the expansion of the railways. It was possible to reach Penzance from 1859, and places like St Ives, Newquay and Looe soon had branch lines – but the main purpose in building them was goods traffic. The real growth of rail tourism began in the 1890s, by which time Bude as well as Newquay were connected, and

Padstow harbour

there were horse bus services from the nearest station to Tintagel or Lizard Town. Padstow got its station in 1899. The famous GWR posters of the 1920s and 1930s promised access to 'the Cornish Riviera'. Cornwall was too distant for day trippers, which affected the kind of development which followed.

By 1930, car ownership and better roads meant easier access to a wider area. Within living memory the M5 and the improved A30 have made Cornwall ever more accessible, and tourism is now the mainstay of the local economy.

At the same time, the attractions of owning a second home in Cornwall also increased, especially with the possibility of letting it out during the season. At the time of writing, council tax is due to be increased to discourage second-home purchases.

Many people who fall in love with Cornwall while on holiday are attracted to living full time in Cornwall after retirement, and the new possibilities of remote working mean that some people who are still working can also now make the move. House prices have risen rapidly in consequence.

All this has had an effect on the Cornish economy. There are too many seasonal jobs, many of them low paid even in season. Incomes are low, and it is increasingly difficult for the low-paid and insecure workforce to find anywhere to live. For young people born in Cornwall, there are tough choices to be made: many decide to leave. The hospitality industry finds it difficult to recruit staff.

Despite the income tourism generates, Cornwall is poor. In 2018 it was listed as the second poorest region in the whole of northern Europe, and used to receive financial help from the EU. The poverty is scarcely noticeable to most visitors, however.

Porthcurno beach

Some other 'differences'

Gardens

Cornwall's climate is different from the rest of Britain, due to the Gulf Stream and vicinity to the ocean. Parts of south-west Cornwall are nearly frost-free, and mild winters and warm but not over-hot summers allow plants to grow here which would not thrive even on Cornwall's north coast.

The owners of great estates in this area in the early nineteenth century competed with each other to see who could form the most impressive sub-tropical paradise. They employed botanists and plant-hunters such as the Cornish-born Lobb brothers to bring back exotic plants from acoss the world, including some we now take for granted such as rhododendrons and the monkey-puzzle tree.

Visiting Heligan, Trebah (photo above) or Glendurgan is something which makes Cornwall special even to non-horticulturalists.

Myths and legends

Most areas of Britain have their own folklore, but not all were equally lucky in finding Victorian folklore enthusiasts to collect it. Cornwall had a number, led by William Bottrell and Robert Hunt, the former being a great collector, the latter being a better writer. Because it was 'a land apart', with a different cultural history, their stories of giants and mermaids, piskies and witches, are particularly intriguing.

Seemingly quite separate from the main body of Cornish folklore, there are the Arthurian legends which centre on Tintagel, though there are other places to visit too, along with the story of Tristan and Iseult. These legends seem to have their origins in medieval Breton or Norman writers, rather than Cornish sources. A major boost to the Arthur story (and to Tintagel as a destination) came with Tennyson's *Idylls of the King* in 1859, and then Robert Hawker's *Quest of the Sangraal* in 1864.

Artists' colonies

In the 1880s, Newlyn attracted artists who were looking for an equivalent of the French *en plein air* school. Newlyn attracted them because of the quality of the light, because they were fascinated by the active fishing community, and probably because it was cheap. Among the first to settle was Walter Langley, but the most famous members were Stanhope Forbes and his wife Elizabeth née Armstrong who settled in Newlyn.

The 'Newlyn School' also took in the neighbouring village of Lamorna, where 'Lamorna' Birch lived. Other well-known names include Laura and Harold Knight, Frank Bramley and Dod Procter.

St Ives had a similar allure. Apparently the decline of the pilchard industry led to artists converting fishermen's abandoned net lofts into studios, especially after the arrival of the railway in 1877. Many of the artists had good connections with London institutions and galleries, and railway carriages were hired to take paintings for exhibiting or sale. Whistler and Sickert arrived in 1884. A school of painting was established, visited by students from many countries.

After the end of WW1 the St Ives School grew, with Bernard Leach setting up a pottery to add variety. Ben Nicholson first visited in 1928,

St Ives

when he met the remarkable local artist Alfred Wallis, and settled in the town with his wife Barbara Hepworth in 1939. After WW2 a large number of young painters arrived, including Peter Lanyon, Patrick Heron and Wilhelmina Barns-Graham.

The Tate St Ives arrived in 1993, and together with the Barbara Hepworth Museum and Sculpture Garden, has made the town a centre for art appreciation.

Of course Cornwall was not 'different' in having artists' colonies. There were a number in France, and the fishing town of Kirkcudbright in south-west Scotland developed a colony at much the same time as Newlyn and St Ives.

But whilst each of Cornwall's 'differences' may have comparable equivalents elsewhere, taken together they amount to 'a land apart'.

If you want to know where to see the finest examples of Cornwall's 'differences', I suggest you read *101 Things to See in Cornwall* by Robert Hesketh.

Other Bossiney books you may find interesting

101 Things to see in Cornwall
Brunel in the West
Cornish engineers and inventors
Cornwall and slavery
Cornwall's railway heritage
Cornwall's writers
Druids in the South-West?
King Arthur – man or myth?
King Arthur's footsteps
Remarkable women of Cornwall
Tales of Cornish giants
Tales of Cornish mariners and mermaids
Tales of Cornish witchcraft
Traditional Cornish recipes
Walking North Cornwall to Dartmoor in 1854

Walks books

Really short walks – North Cornwall
Really short walks – St Ives to Padstow
Really short walks – West Cornwall
Shortish walks – Bodmin Moor
Shortish walks near the Land's End
Shortish walks on and around the Lizard
Shortish walks – North Cornwall
Shortish walks – Lower Tamar valley
Writers' walks on the Cornish coast

Guide books

About Tintagel
Cornwall beach and cove guide: North coast
Cornwall beach and cove guide: South coast
Discover North Cornwall
The Lizard peninsula
Penzance to Land's End